Did You Hear Wind Sing Your Name?

An Oneida Song of Spring

Sandra
De Coteau
Orie

ILLUSTRATIONS BY

*Christopher
Canyon*

MONDO

Elements of nature are personified in the Oneida culture to reflect the people's deep relationship with the natural world. Capitalization in the text reflects this tradition.

The illustrations on the opening pages are the artist's representation of Oneida beadwork, which is the traditional form of artistic expression for the Oneida people.

This edition published in the United States of America in 1997
by MONDO Publishing
First published in the United States of America in 1995 by Walker Publishing Company, Inc.

Printed in Hong Kong. First Mondo printing, October 1996
01 02 03 04 05   9 8 7 6 5 4 3

ISBN 1-57255-199-2

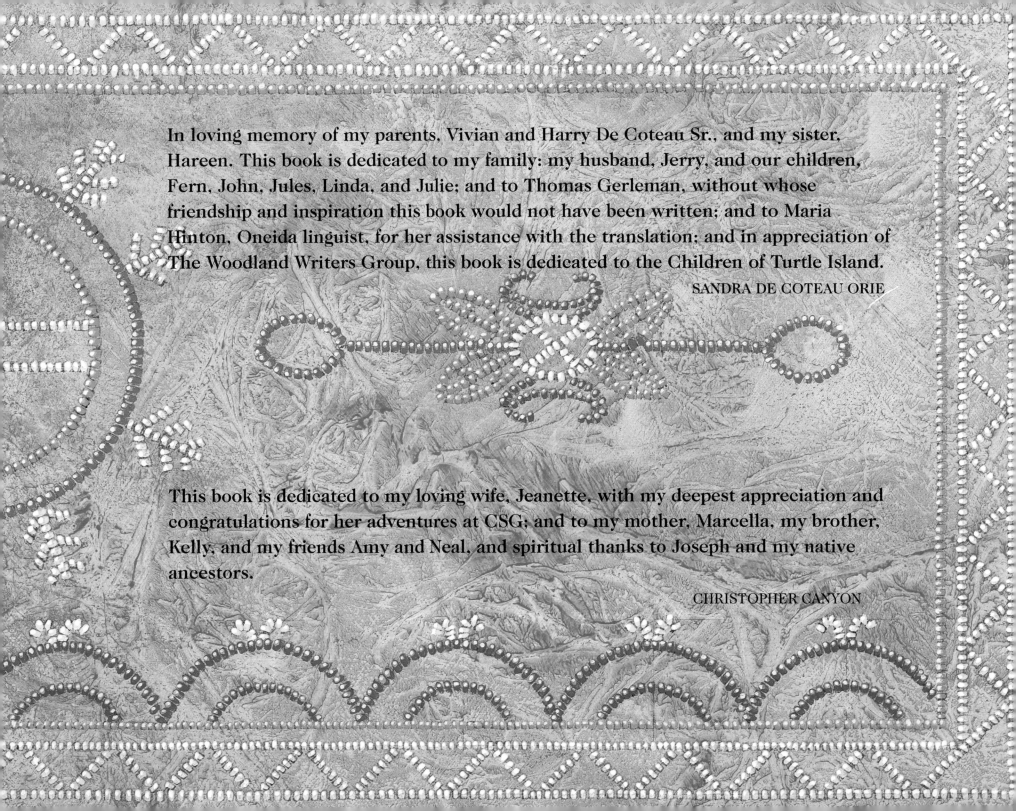

In loving memory of my parents, Vivian and Harry De Coteau Sr., and my sister, Hareen. This book is dedicated to my family: my husband, Jerry, and our children, Fern, John, Jules, Linda, and Julie; and to Thomas Gerleman, without whose friendship and inspiration this book would not have been written; and to Maria Hinton, Oneida linguist, for her assistance with the translation; and in appreciation of The Woodland Writers Group, this book is dedicated to the Children of Turtle Island.

SANDRA DE COTEAU ORIE

This book is dedicated to my loving wife, Jeanette, with my deepest appreciation and congratulations for her adventures at CSG; and to my mother, Marcella, my brother, Kelly, and my friends Amy and Neal, and spiritual thanks to Joseph and my native ancestors.

CHRISTOPHER CANYON

Author's Note

This book reflects the deep relationship Oneida people have with the natural world. It is a celebration of the circle of life, of the return of morning to night as well as of each cycle of the seasons.

The elements of nature you will read about symbolize our relationship with nature. The Pine tree represents the unity of the Six Nations of the Iroquois Confederacy: the Oneida, Mohawk, Seneca, Cayuga, Onondaga, and Tuscarora. The tree's great white roots extend to all Six Nations.

The Oneida also believe in the importance of the Hawk, the bringer of good news, of our strength-giving Elder Brother Sun, and of recognizing the Cedar and Sweet Grass used in our ceremonies.

The Three Sisters—Corn, Beans, and Squash—are very important to Oneida people. They are the staple crops that have sustained us and have helped the Oneida survive.

The flowers give us beauty, and they announce Spring's arrival. The Trilliums are the first flowers of the woodlands, and the Strawberries are the first fruits of the season.

This book is a song about the approach of Spring, and in the Oneida language, to sing means to give thanks. You are invited to join in this thanksgiving.

Traveling North
Did you see
Spirit Hawk dancing on the Wind?

Did you feel
morning Sun's warmth upon your face
welcoming you to a new day?

Did you see
the White Birch standing tall among the Darkwoods
and the greening of the Aspen Saplings?

Did you smell
the sweet scent of the sacred Cedar?

Did you see the fields of the Three Sisters coming?

Did you see
Sun's face in the Buttercup?
And did you see Sky's blue in the wildwood Violets?

Did you greet
the Four-leggeds
and celebrate the Winged-One's
dances?

Did you trace
Turtle's tracks along the Creek
and know you weren't alone?

*D*id you hear
Wind sing your name?
Does your memory bring Sweet Grass's fragrance?

Did you taste
the Thunderer's moist sky Waters?
Were you healed by Meadow's wild
Strawberries?

Did your eyes catch Sunset's burgundy?
Did you see Trillium's Stars
lying upon the Forest bed's heaven?

Did you sense Grandmother Moon guiding you home again?

Did your heart
bring home the songs of all These living?

Did you, along with These, travel this sacred circle called Spring?